CW00493641

Tibet

A traveler's guide book

White L Mill

Table of content

Local dishes in Tibet

Chapter 1

Geography and Climate

Tibet, commonly referred to as the "Roof of the World," is a mesmerizing location tucked amid the Himalayas. Its distinctive topography contains huge stretches of magnificent landscapes, high mountain ranges, and flowing rivers that define its particular character. Embarking on a tour in Tibet means immersing oneself in a place of exceptional natural beauty and awe-inspiring geography.

Stretching over an area of roughly 1.2 million square kilometers, Tibet is situated on the Tibetan Plateau, one of the highest and biggest plateaus in the world. Its average height surpasses 4,000 meters, giving it a site of remarkable altitude and magnificence. The area is bordered by huge mountain ranges, including the beautiful Himalayas to the south, the Kunlun Mountains to the north, and the Karakoram Range to the west. These gigantic mountain obstacles have sheltered Tibet from most of the outside world, maintaining its unique cultural and natural legacy.

The Himalayas, associated with Tibet, dominate the southern region with their snow-capped peaks and rugged beauty. This iconic mountain range comprises many of the world's tallest peaks, including Mount Everest, known as "Chomolungma" in Tibetan, rising at an awe-inspiring height of 8,848 meters. Other noteworthy Himalayan peaks in Tibet are Cho Oyu, Makalu, and Shishapangma, each towering tall with its distinct attractiveness. The Himalayas not only enchant their beauty but also play a significant role in influencing the region's climate and water supplies.

Tibet is endowed with a complex network of rivers that meander over its vast territory, springing from the snow-capped mountains and glaciers. The area is the source of several important rivers in Asia, including the great Yangtze (known as the "Drechu" in Tibetan), the

Yellow River (known as the "Ma Chu"), the Mekong River (known as the "Lancang River"), and the Brahmaputra River (known as the "Yarlung Tsangpo"). These rivers form vast valleys, affording breathtaking views and lush farmland that support the local population.

As for Tibet's climate, it is largely impacted by its high altitude and peculiar monsoon system. Due to its height, Tibet has a peculiar highland climate marked by low temperatures and dramatic temperature changes. Winters are cold and brutal, with temperatures regularly plunging far below freezing, especially in the upper altitudes. Summers, on the other hand, are generally moderate and short-lived, with daytime temperatures ranging from cold to pleasantly warm.

Tibet's weather patterns are also impacted by the Indian monsoon, which sends heavy rainfall to the area from June to September. During this period, the environment is decked with brilliant foliage, and the rivers surge with rich waters.

Travelers visiting Tibet during the monsoon season should be prepared for periodic showers and organize their activities appropriately.

In addition to the monsoon, the area enjoys a separate dry season from October to May. This era is marked by bright skies, plentiful sunlight, and low humidity. However, the weather may be rather frigid, particularly during the winter months, so tourists must dress properly and be prepared for the cold.

It is worth mentioning that owing to the high altitude, tourists visiting Tibet may encounter the symptoms of altitude sickness, often known as acute mountain sickness (AMS). Symptoms may include headache, dizziness, nausea, and shortness of breath. It is essential to adapt gradually to the altitude, remain hydrated, and seek medical treatment if required.

In conclusion, Tibet's topography provides a stunning combination of huge landscapes, high mountain ranges, and flowing rivers. Its spectacular beauty, along with its particular temperature and seasonal fluctuations, makes it a destination like no other. Travelers traveling into Tibet should prepare themselves for the high altitude, variable temperatures, and the risk of meeting rains during the monsoon season. Embracing the awe-inspiring character of Tibet demands both an awareness of its geographical grandeur and proper preparedness for the climatic conditions that define this amazing place.

Chapter 2

Cultural and Historical Background

Tibet, a nation steeped in a rich cultural and historical legacy, draws travelers with its intriguing customs and deep spirituality. From its ancient monasteries and colorful festivals to its exquisite art and awe-inspiring architecture, Tibet looks at a distinct and dynamic Tibetan culture that has existed for generations.

At the center of Tibetan culture lies Buddhism, which has played a key influence in establishing the region's identity. The arrival of Buddhism to Tibet may be traced back to the 7th century, under the reign of King Songtsen Gampo. The king's marital partnerships with Nepalese and Chinese princesses introduced Buddhist influence to the area, and he is credited with laying the basis for the expansion of Buddhism in Tibet. Subsequently, the famous Buddhist teacher Padmasambhava, better known as Guru

Rinpoche, came to Tibet in the 8th century and played a vital role in establishing Buddhism as the prevailing religion.

Buddhism in Tibet is largely practiced in its Vajrayana form, often known as Tibetan Buddhism. This spiritual tradition mixes parts of Mahayana Buddhism with indigenous Tibetan traditions, providing a unique mixture of teachings and rituals. Tibetan Buddhism lays a significant focus on meditation, spiritual enlightenment, and the search for inner peace. Monasteries, typically located in distant and attractive areas, serve as centers of spiritual instruction, where monks dedicate their lives to study, contemplation, and the preservation of Buddhist teachings.

The monastic institution in Tibet has been crucial to the preservation and dissemination of Tibetan culture. Monasteries, such as the renowned Potala Palace in Lhasa, function as architectural wonders and possess tremendous historical and theological value. These vast temples, covered with exquisite paintings, sculptures, and texts, are not only places of prayer but also stores of knowledge and art.

Tibetan art represents the profound spiritual and cultural legacy of the area. Thangka paintings, marked by detailed intricacies and brilliant hues, portray deities, mandalas, and scenes from Buddhist texts. These portable art pieces serve as aids to meditation and are commonly shown during religious activities. Sculptures, both great and little, made with careful precision, decorate monasteries and temples, presenting visual images of enlightened beings and motivating devotees in their spiritual activities.

Traditional Tibetan rituals and festivals are colorful representations of the region's cultural identity. Losar, the Tibetan New Year, is a festive event highlighted by colorful processions, music, dancing, and traditional rituals aimed at banishing bad energy and bringing in good fortune. Saga Dawa, another famous festival, celebrates the birth, enlightenment, and death of

Buddha, bringing visitors from far and wide to holy locations like Mount Kailash and the Jokhang Temple.

Tibetan traditions and etiquette are profoundly based on respect and compassion. The customary greeting, "Tashi Delek," coupled with a short bow, denotes good luck and well-wishes. Tibetan hospitality is legendary, with travelers frequently greeted with a warm cup of butter tea and traditional Tibetan foods, reflecting the region's nomadic background.

Historically, Tibet has experienced the emergence and fall of different dynasties and the ebb and flow of political power. The era of Tibetan history commonly associated with independence and wealth is known as the Tibetan Empire, which lasted from the 7th through the 9th century. Subsequently, the province fell under the control of different Mongol and Chinese emperors, resulting in fluctuating political landscapes.

The 13th and 14th centuries witnessed the development of the famed Tibetan spiritual leader, the Dalai Lama. The Dalai Lamas, considered to be the reincarnations of Avalokiteshvara, the Bodhisattva of Compassion, were significant leaders in both religious and political sectors. The Fifth Dalai Lama, Ngawang Lobsang Gyatso, united Tibet and founded the Ganden Phodrang regime, which lasted until the Chinese invasion in the mid-20th century.

In 1950, the People's Republic of China invaded Tibet, resulting in tremendous political and cultural turmoil. The ensuing Chinese occupation led to the persecution of Tibetan Buddhism and the degradation of traditional Tibetan culture. However, Tibetan culture and spirituality have persevered, and the preservation efforts by Tibetans both inside and beyond Tibet have helped keep the torch of Tibetan history alive.

In conclusion, Tibet's cultural and historical history is a treasure trove that captivates with its spirituality, art, architecture, and ancient rituals. The deep impact of Buddhism, the lively festivals, the exquisite artworks, and the long history of the Tibetan people have formed a unique culture that continues to survive among the difficulties of the contemporary world. Exploring Tibet is an invitation to immerse oneself in a mesmerizing tapestry of spirituality and culture, where ancient knowledge and deep beauty mix to create an experience like no other.

Chapter 3

Travel Permits and Regulations

Tibet, owing to its political position and sensitivity, has unique procedures in place for anyone intending to visit the area. These restrictions attempt to limit the influx of visitors and ensure stability in the area. It is crucial for travelers to understand the process of getting the requisite permissions and to be informed of any limits, entrance criteria, and rules for their visit to Tibet.

The principal permission necessary for going to Tibet is the Tibet Travel permission, commonly known as the Tibet Entry Permit or Tibet Tourism Bureau (TTB) permit. This permission is given by the Tibet Tourism Bureau and is an obligatory requirement for all non-Chinese tourists visiting Tibet. The permission is normally acquired via a travel firm authorized to handle the permit application procedure.

To apply for the Tibet Travel Permit, tourists need to organize a trip through a recognized travel firm that specializes in Tibet tourism. The agency will aid in the permission application procedure and plan an itinerary that conforms with the rules imposed by the government. It is vital to know that individual travel is not authorized in Tibet, and all passengers must be part of an organized trip.

To receive the Tibet Travel Permit, passengers needed to give specific papers to the travel agency, including a scanned copy of their passport and Chinese visa. It is necessary to apply for permission well in advance since the processing period might take several weeks. The travel agency will handle the permit application and contact passengers once permission is issued. The original permission is normally handed to the traveler's accommodation in mainland China or Tibet before their departure.

In addition to the Tibet Travel Permit, some restricted locations in Tibet may need an Alien's Travel Permit (ATP). The ATP is given by the Public Security Bureau (PSB) and is necessary for travel to locations such as Everest Base Camp, Mount Kailash, and some border areas. The ATP application is normally handled by the travel agency as part of the entire permission procedure. It is vital to remember that passengers cannot apply for the ATP alone and must be part of an organized tour to receive this authorization.

For some sensitive locations in Tibet, such as military zones and closed border sections, a Military Permit is needed. The Military Permit is acquired by the local military office and may only be provided by the travel operator in consultation with the right authorities. Travelers should contact their travel agent about the necessity for a Military Permit depending on their intended itinerary.

Tourists must comply with the norms and limits established by the government throughout their stay in Tibet. This includes staying in registered hotels, traveling solely with authorized guides, and following the approved itinerary. Visitors should also be aware of any prohibitions on photography and respect the religious and cultural customs of the local community.

Entry into Tibet is available via several ways, including flights from major Chinese cities and adjacent countries, as well as rail travels from mainland China. It is vital to examine the newest entrance criteria, such as visa laws and health-related procedures, since they may differ and are subject to change.

In conclusion, owing to its political sensitivity, Tibet has unique laws in place for tourists. Obtaining the requisite licenses, including the Tibet Travel Permit, Alien's Travel Permit, and Military Permit (if applicable), is a critical element of the procedure. Travelers should cooperate with approved travel agents to manage the permit application procedure and guarantee compliance with the criteria and limits imposed by the authorities. Being informed of admission criteria, limits, and norms is vital for a smooth and successful visit to this unique and culturally significant location.

Chapter 4

Major Cities and Attractions

Nestled within the gorgeous landscapes of Tibet, various renowned places draw tourists with their distinct charm and rich cultural history. From the busy city of Lhasa to the calm landscapes of Shigatse, Gyantse, and the holy Mount Kailash, each destination provides an exceptional experience replete with significant monuments, old monasteries, palaces, and spectacular natural marvels.

Lhasa, the pulsing heart of Tibet, draws tourists with its grandeur and spiritual importance. In the middle of the city rises the spectacular Potala Palace, an architectural masterpiece that looms above Lhasa. This UNESCO World Heritage site was originally the winter palace of the Dalai Lamas and shows the subtleties of Tibetan art and culture. With its towering white walls and golden roofs, the castle is a sight to see, holding churches, prayer rooms, and rare treasures.

Jokhang Temple, a spiritual sanctuary located in the center of Lhasa, is a key pilgrimage place for Tibetan Buddhists. This respected sanctuary, bordered by the busy Barkhor Street, radiates a feeling of tranquillity. Inside, the atmosphere is filled with the perfume of incense and the sound of chanting worshippers. The temple's architecture, embellished with vivid colors and complex embellishments, captivates tourists as they see the dedication and spiritual traditions of the Tibetan people.

Shigatse, the second-largest city in Tibet, is home to the famed Tashilhunpo Monastery. This historic monastery, constructed by the First Dalai Lama, is an architectural wonder and the seat of the Panchen Lama. The centerpiece of Tashilhunpo is the huge Maitreya Buddha statue, rising at an astonishing 26 meters in height. As visitors tour the monastery's different chapels, they are enveloped in a world of religious devotion, filled with magnificent murals and carefully sculpted sculptures.

In the village of Gyantse, the Kumbum Stupa stands as a tribute to the region's rich history and creative genius. This multi-tiered tower, also known as the Gyantse Kumbum, is a remarkable example of Tibetan Buddhist architecture. Each story of the stupa includes beautiful paintings, illustrating religious legends and heavenly entities. Climbing to the summit provides tourists with panoramic views of the town and neighboring countryside.

Mount Kailash, a holy mountain in western Tibet, carries great importance for numerous faiths. This gorgeous mountain, considered to be the home of deities, draws travelers from many religions. The ancient pilgrimage around Mount Kailash, known as the Kora, is a revered spiritual trek done by followers seeking blessings and enlightenment. The rugged beauty of the surrounding surroundings, including turquoise lakes and wide valleys, contributes to the awe-inspiring experience.

Tibet is endowed with natural treasures that leave tourists in awe of its magnificence. Namtso Lake, sometimes referred to as the "Heavenly Lake," is one such jewel. Surrounded by snow-capped mountains, the lake's peaceful waters mirror the ever-changing hues of the sky. It is a paradise for photographers and environment aficionados, delivering a feeling of calm and beauty that is hard to find anywhere.

Yamdrok Lake, popularly known as the "Turquoise Lake," mesmerizes with its bright blue colors and majestic mountain background. Traveling along its coastlines, travelers are treated to stunning panoramas that appear as paintings come to life. The lake bears significant spiritual importance for Tibetans and gives a feeling of peace among nature's majesty.

Each of these prominent sites in Tibet allows guests to immerse themselves in the region's significant cultural history and natural beauties. From the towering monuments of Lhasa, Shigatse, and Gyantse to the spiritual trip around Mount Kailash and the enchanting beauty of Namtso and Yamdrok lakes, discovering these sites is an invitation to see the remarkable and feel the essence of Tibet in all its magnificence.

Chapter 5

Transportation and Accommodation

Traveling in Tibet provides many kinds of transportation, including aircraft, trains, and road excursions, each giving distinct experiences and chances to immerse oneself in the region's awe-inspiring surroundings. Whether you choose to fly, go on a picturesque train excursion, or choose for road travel, smart preparation, and attention may guarantee a pleasant and pleasurable experience.

Flights are a practical and time-efficient method to visit Tibet. Gonggar Airport in Lhasa is the principal entrance point, with flights linking major Chinese cities such as Beijing, Shanghai, Chengdu, and Kathmandu in Nepal. It is suggested to book flights in advance, since availability might be restricted, particularly during high travel seasons. It's crucial to remember that owing to the high altitude, flights to Tibet may be susceptible to weather conditions, so it's smart to have a flexible travel itinerary.

If you want a more immersive and picturesque vacation, traveling by train is a popular alternative. The Qinghai-Tibet Railway, one of the tallest and most spectacular railroads in the world, links major Chinese cities including Beijing, Shanghai, Chengdu, and Xining to Lhasa. The train trip provides breathtaking sights of the Tibetan Plateau, snow-capped mountains, and huge grasslands. It's advised to reserve rail tickets well in advance since they tend to sell out rapidly. To acclimatize to the high altitude, it's advisable to select a sleeper bed and ensure you keep hydrated during the trip.

Road travel in Tibet offers a more flexible and immersive experience, as it enables possibilities to explore distant locations and appreciate the spectacular vistas at your speed. Hiring a private car or joining a guided trip is a frequent strategy. The itineraries might vary based on the exact sites you choose to visit, but popular excursions include the Friendship Highway from Lhasa to Kathmandu, the road from Lhasa to Shigatse, and the picturesque drive to Mount Kailash. It's crucial to find a reputable driver and ensure the car is in excellent condition for lengthy drives over often tough terrain.

When it comes to lodgings in Tibet, there are alternatives to fit all interests and budgets. In important towns like Lhasa and Shigatse, you'll discover a selection of hotels, from luxury places to budget-friendly alternatives. These hotels frequently offer nice facilities and cater to varied demands. It's important to book lodgings in advance, particularly during high travel seasons, to ensure your favorite selections.

For a more immersive experience, staying in guesthouses or Tibetan-owned family-run facilities may give a greater connection to local culture and customs. These hotels frequently create a warm and inviting environment, providing tourists the chance to connect with local hosts and acquire insights into Tibetan everyday life.

In more distant places or during hiking adventures, camping may be an exciting and rewarding alternative. It enables you to be immersed in the natural splendor of Tibet and enjoy its calm sceneries firsthand. It's crucial to ensure you have sufficient camping gear, including a robust tent, comfortable sleeping bags, and proper insulation to resist the frigid temperatures at high elevations. Additionally, getting essential licenses for camping in specific regions may be needed, so it's important to check with local officials or travel firms ahead.

When traveling in Tibet, it's vital to prepare correctly for the varying weather conditions and high altitudes. Layered clothes, suitable walking shoes, sunscreen, and sunglasses are advised. It's also important to bring the required medicines, as well as drink lots of water and take appropriate rest to adapt to the altitude gradually.

In conclusion, Tibet provides many kinds of transportation, including aircraft, trains, and road excursions, each with its own merits. Careful planning, scheduling in advance, and choosing appropriate hotels contribute to a pleasant and happy vacation experience. Whether you prefer to experience the region's attractions by air, immerse yourself in the gorgeous train trip, or embark on an exciting road tour, Tibet's awe-inspiring landscapes and rich cultural legacy await your discovery.

Chapter 6

Outdoor Activities and Trekking

Tibet, with its beautiful scenery and awe-inspiring mountain ranges, is a refuge for outdoor lovers seeking exhilarating activities in the lap of nature. The area provides a plethora of chances for activities such as hiking, climbing, and camping, delivering wonderful experiences for explorers of all levels of ability.

Trekking in Tibet enables tourists to immerse themselves in the region's unspoiled natural splendor and discover distant locations that are unreachable by other means. One of the most famous hiking routes is the Everest Base Camp trip. This tough but rewarding route takes you through magnificent valleys, attractive towns, and mountainous terrain, affording amazing views of Mount Everest and other towering peaks along the way. The walk normally starts at Rongbuk Monastery, the highest monastery in the world, and proceeds to the North Base Camp of Everest.

For those wanting a less rigorous trekking experience, the Ganden to Samye trip is a wonderful alternative. This beautiful journey takes you through the gorgeous sceneries of the Kyichu Valley, passing by various monasteries and steep mountain passes. The walk gives an insight into Tibetan culture, with the opportunity to engage with local locals and explore old monastery structures.

Safety is crucial while conducting any adventurous activity in Tibet. It is vital to acclimatize adequately to the high altitude before beginning a journey. Gradual climbing and giving time for relaxation are vital to prevent altitude sickness. It's recommended to contact expert guides or local authorities to ensure you have a safe and fun trekking trip.

Proper equipment is crucial for hiking in Tibet. Sturdy and comfortable trekking boots, warm and layered clothes appropriate for varied weather conditions, a decent quality sleeping bag, a waterproof backpack, and trekking poles are among the important equipment to consider. Additionally, packing a first aid kit, sunscreen, a hat, sunglasses, and extra water and food is vital for a safe and pleasurable walk.

Mountaineering aficionados will find many possibilities in Tibet, with its several high peaks and demanding summits. Mount Everest, the world's tallest peak, is a goal for many mountaineers. However, climbing Everest takes substantial mountaineering knowledge, physical fitness, and specific equipment. It is vital to join an organized expedition with professional guides and support personnel to assure safety and success.

For individuals with intermediate climbing ability, peaks like Cho Oyu and Shishapangma provide tough but doable goals. These mountains give a chance to experience the excitement of high-altitude climbing and observe the breathtaking panoramic vistas from their summits. It is important to perform rigorous training and acclimatization before attempting such climbs and to join reliable climbing expeditions.

Camping in Tibet gives a unique chance to immerse oneself in the region's pristine landscapes and star-filled sky. Whether in the proximity of holy lakes like Namtso or among the rugged grandeur of the Himalayas, camping allows for a deeper touch with nature. When camping, it is vital to have adequate camping gear, including a durable tent, comfortable sleeping bags, insulated mats, and cooking equipment. Additionally, acquiring relevant licenses and following local restrictions for camping in specified regions is crucial.

Recommended itineraries for hiking and climbing vary dependent on the selected route and individual preferences. It is important to provide adequate time for acclimatization, relaxation days, and flexibility in case of unforeseen weather circumstances. Consulting with expert local guides and travel firms may give significant insights into arranging appropriate itineraries that correspond with your interests and experience level.

In conclusion, Tibet provides stunning vistas and exhilarating prospects for outdoor lovers. Whether walking through valleys, ascending towering peaks, or camping beneath starry nights, travelers are blessed with options. Safety precautions, adequate equipment, and acclimatization are crucial while beginning these expeditions. With careful preparation, competent guides, and a spirit of adventure, Tibet delivers remarkable experiences that will leave outdoor enthusiasts in awe of its natural beauty.

Chapter 7

Cuisine and local dishes

Tibetan cuisine is a lovely expression of the region's cultural history and distinct tastes. From substantial traditional meals to modern adaptations, the food of Tibet tantalizes the taste buds with its unique ingredients and tastes, all while exhibiting the region's rich culinary heritage.

One of the major elements of Tibetan cuisine is barley, which flourishes in the tough conditions of the area. Barley is used to create tsampa, a staple meal in Tibetan homes. Tsampa is created by toasting barley flour and blending it with butter tea, resulting in a dough-like consistency that is nourishing and invigorating.

Yak meat is another significant component in Tibetan recipes, due to the ubiquity of yak rearing in the area. Yak meat is noted for its rich taste and is widely used in stews, momos (Tibetan dumplings), and different meat-based meals. The flesh is tender and lends a particular flavor to the meals.

Tibetan noodles, known as thukpa, are a favorite comfort meal. These hand-pulled noodles are generally served in a rich broth with veggies and meat, creating a full and fulfilling meal. Thenthuk, a similar noodle dish, includes thicker noodles and is especially popular in the Amdo and Kham districts of Tibet.

Another well-loved Tibetan meal is momo, a sort of dumpling stuffed with meat or veggies. Momo is often steamed or fried and served with a sour dipping sauce. These delectable dumplings are a popular street meal and can be found in many cafes in Tibet.

Butter tea, known as po cha, is a distinctive Tibetan beverage. It is produced by churning yak butter with strong tea and adding a bit of salt. The final drink has a creamy texture and a somewhat salty flavor. Butter tea is not only loved for its peculiar taste but also provides a source of warmth and vitality in the chilly Tibetan environment.

When it comes to luxury dining in Tibet, various locations provide sophisticated gastronomic experiences. In Lhasa, the capital city, Makye Ame and Shang Palace are famous luxury restaurants. Makye Ame offers an attractive ambiance and specializes in Tibetan and foreign fusion food. Shang Palace, situated in the Shangri-La Hotel, serves a choice of scrumptious Chinese and Tibetan delicacies in a refined atmosphere.

Exploring native Tibetan food in traditional settings is also a great experience. In Lhasa, Barkhor Street is a buzzing center where tourists may experience real Tibetan snacks and street cuisine. From freshly cooked momos to scented thukpa, the street is dotted with tiny restaurants and tea shops that provide a range of local delicacies.

As you move beyond Lhasa, the marketplaces in Shigatse and Gyantse also give a taste of native Tibetan food. These colorful marketplaces are full of sellers offering fresh vegetables, local spices, and traditional delicacies. It is a fantastic chance to try regional delicacies and explore the colorful culinary culture of Tibet.

Tibetan food entices with its unusual tastes, powerful ingredients, and cultural relevance. From the ancient mainstays like tsampa and momos to the innovative inventions seen in premium restaurants, the food of Tibet provides a broad spectrum of flavors and textures. Whether relishing a formal dining experience in Lhasa or experiencing the local street food scene, tourists visiting Tibet have the option to engage in a gastronomic adventure that exhibits the region's rich culinary history.

Chapter 8

Practical Tips and Etiquette

When arranging a trip to Tibet, it is vital to consider practical advice and recommendations to guarantee a smooth and pleasurable journey. Here are some important ideas to help you prepare for your journey:

Packing Essentials:

Layered clothes: Tibet's weather may be unpredictable, so bring a range of clothing alternatives to adapt to diverse temperatures and weather situations.
Comfortable walking shoes: Ensure you have strong shoes for walking and touring numerous sights, as well as comfortable footwear for daily usage.
Sun protection: Tibet's high altitude means greater sun rays, so carry sunscreen, a hat, and

sunglasses to protect yourself from UV radiation.

treatments: Consult with your healthcare practitioner about altitude sickness treatments and carry a basic first aid kit with vital prescriptions.

Water bottle: Staying hydrated is vital at high elevations, so pack a reusable water bottle and refill it often with clean drinking water.

Altitude Sickness Prevention and Management:

Acclimatization: Take time to acclimatize to the high altitude by resting and avoiding intense activity upon arrival. Gradually raise your exercise level over a few days.

Hydration: Drink lots of water to keep hydrated and avoid altitude sickness. Avoid excessive alcohol and caffeine consumption.

Diet: Consume small, easily digested meals and avoid heavy, fatty foods during the early days of acclimation.

drugs: Consult with your healthcare professional about using drugs to prevent or treat altitude sickness. Follow their advice thoroughly.

Local Etiquette and Interacting with Locals:

pleasantries: Learn simple Tibetan pleasantries like "Tashi Delek" (meaning "good luck") and greet people with a smile and a small nod or bow.

Respect cultural norms: Tibetans are profoundly religious, therefore show respect while visiting monasteries, temples, and other important locations. Dress modestly, remove your shoes when requested, and observe any directions or limitations.

Photography: Seek permission before photographing persons, religious items, or rituals. Be sensitive to cultural sensitivities and respect people's privacy.

Language: Learn a few basic Tibetan words or carry a phrasebook to enhance conversation and show respect for the local culture.

Responsible Tourism:

Eco-friendly practices: Respect the environment by disposing of garbage correctly and avoiding littering. Carry a reusable bag for shopping and avoid using single-use plastics.

Cultural sensitivity: Be cognizant of local customs and traditions. Seek authorization before handling religious objects or visiting restricted areas.

Support local businesses: Choose locally owned lodgings, restaurants, and stores to contribute to the local economy and receive a more genuine experience.

Responsible trekking: Follow authorized paths, protect animals and natural environments, and leave no trace. Obtain appropriate permissions and abide by local restrictions for hiking and camping.

Remember, traveling safely and respecting local culture will improve your experience in Tibet and help the preservation of its cultural and natural treasures. Embrace the chance to learn from and participate in the local community, building cross-cultural understanding and respect.

Printed in Great Britain
by Amazon

30444360R00026